DR. SHINICHI SUZUKI
Teaching Music from the Heart

DR. SHINICHI SUZUKI
Teaching Music from the Heart

David R. Collins

MORGAN
REYNOLDS
Publishers, Inc.
620 South Elm Street, Suite 223
Greensboro, North Carolina 27406
http://www.morganreynolds.com

DR. SHINICHI SUZUKI: TEACHING MUSIC FROM THE HEART

Library of Congress Cataloging-in-Publication Data

Collins, David R.
    Dr. Shinichi Suzuki : teaching music from the heart / David R. Collins.
        p. cm.
    Includes bibliographical references and index.
    Summary: A biography of the Japanese violin teacher who developed the Suzuki
Method, a way of teaching children how to play certain instruments at a very
early age.
    ISBN 1-883846-49-8 (lib. bdg.)
    1. Suzuki, Shin'ichi, 1898---Juvenile literature. 2. Music
teachers--Japan--Biography--Juvenile literature. [1. Suzuki, Shin'ichi, 1898- 2. Music
teachers.] I. Title.

ML3930.S988 C65 2001
780'.92--dc21
[B]
                                                                2001040194

Printed in the United States of America
First Edition

*The Publisher wishes to dedicate this book
to the memory of
David R. Collins, 1940-2001*

Contents

Dr. Shinichi Suzuki believed that all children were capable of great things if given the opportunity to cultivate their talents. *(Photograph © Arthur Montzka.)*

Chapter One

Mischief Maker

Young Shinichi Suzuki was a real *itazurakko*. For those who do not know Japanese, the word means "a mischievous boy." Shinichi bowed respectfully before his elders and he tried hard to keep his room clean. He took time to write every Japanese character clearly in his classes. Yet, often his father and mother shook their heads at their young son. He was truly full of mischief.

Shinichi's brothers and sisters understood not to run around their house that was filled with ornate vases and other pottery. For centuries, the city of Nagoya, Japan, had been acclaimed for its elegant chinaware. Masakichi Suzuki, a respected violin maker, owned a fine home that he filled with expensive porcelains and ceramics. Chest high vases stood at doorways, handpainted plates hung on brackets, decorating the walls, and sculpted figurines sat on tables. Most young boys would have taken extra care in a house so full of breakables.

But Shinichi Suzuki was not like most young boys. Shinichi seemed to have an extra bit of energy. From the moment he was born on October 18, 1898, he showed signs of a special zest for living. He wiggled when he was held. His cries were full volume and frequent. He craved attention, never wanting to be alone.

"The boy cannot stay still," his father told family friends. "He is always moving. He does not make soft sounds. He roars like a tiger. He is as full of life as any two of my other children." Although the man spoke with a weariness in his voice, there was a hint of pride as well. "Yes. The child bears watching."

Masakichi Suzuki spent as much time watching his young son as he could. Masakichi, like his father, Masaharu, was a maker of musical instruments. Masaharu had been a *samurai*, or a member of the military class of feudal Japan. Masaharu was not well-off. He made *samisen,* a three-stringed Japanese lute, in order to make ends meet. His son, Masakichi, had seen a violin for the first time in 1886. Although the instrument had been brought to Japan 400 years earlier by Christian mission-aries, Emporer Tokuwaga had outlawed them. By 1888, Masakichi was making violins which the new emporer, Meiji, had brought back into popularity.

Although Masakichi personally continued to make violins by hand, in 1900 he began manufacturing his instruments by machine at the Suzuki Violin Factory. Masakichi was a forward-thinking man and also manufactured other Western instruments, such as mandolins and guitars, as the Japanese export market began to flourish. The work kept him at his factory next door for many hours each day. But he wasted no time when he was home, surrounding himself with his sons and teaching them how to live a good life.

Madame Suzuki also came from a *samurai* family, although her father was wealthier than her husband's. Madame Suzuki's maiden name was Ryo Fujie, and as a mother she spent more time with the daughters of the family. She was as small and delicate as many of the vases in their home. Yet her soft voice carried a firmness that demanded attention and respect. She knew much about flowers, gardens, art, and music. She had learned to play the *samisen* as a child. Her pride in her husband's work was clear. "To create beautiful music in a world too often full of sad sounds is a gift," she would say. "A violin carries love and joy in it." Shinichi agreed. But sometimes violins made wonderful toys too—and weapons as well!

As in any family, the Suzuki brothers and sisters fought. Shinichi surprised his brothers with a swift, sudden swat to the posterior with the back of a violin. Even Shinichi's sisters received surprise swats—not as hard—but swats nonetheless. Shinichi learned to make fast getaways, but there were times when he collided with one of the vases and ended up in a long conference with his father.

Masakichi Suzuki saw that his family knew the city of

Nagoya well. Nagoya was called the "Middle Capital," because it sat between the old capital of Kyoto and the present capital city of Tokyo. As Japan's fourth largest city, there were many places to visit. Shinichi's favorite place was Nagoya Castle. Built in 1612 by a Japanese warrior, the sturdy structure with countless rooms and hallways served as a mighty fortress against attackers. As young Shinichi roamed through the castle, he imagined he could hear the cries of soldier attacking soldier and the pounding of cannonballs nearby.

Shinichi's imagination thrived at his father's factory too. Workers often stayed late, polishing the violins until they gleamed in the light of the oil lamp hanging directly above each workplace. To pass the time, the workers told stories of brave Japanese heroes. Often Shinichi joined the men at their work, the small boy sprawling on a mat on the floor. He listened to every word of the storyteller.

"And just as the dragon rose to strike, the grand and glorious warrior Iwami Jutaro leaped from a boulder. Iwami stood up bravely, his eyes gazing ahead at the giant beast."

"Yes? Yes?" young Shinichi burst out, seeking more of the tale.

Following common practice, the storyteller stopped and patted his stomach. "I believe some rice cake would taste well at this time. I need it to continue my story."

Quickly Shinichi sprang to his feet and raced to his home next door. There were always pieces of *mochi* in the big keg in the kitchen. Tossing several handfuls into a bag, the boy hurried back. The storyteller and his friends smiled as they shared the treats. Then, it was back to the tale of the hero Iwami Jutaro, and no one listened with greater interest than Shinichi Suzuki.

There was no doubt where each of the Suzuki sons would attend school. Their father envisioned his sons working in his violin factory, therefore it was only practical to send them to a commercial school in Nagoya. They could study commerce and the principles of economics, and learn how to make the most profit from a manufacturing business. During the summer, the boys could work in the factory itself.

Shinichi followed his father's directions. But, at Nagoya Commercial School, the boy found it hard to study, and his grades showed the results. At the violin factory, he was not afraid of working the more difficult machinery, and muscles formed on his slender frame. Shinichi began to wear glasses early, and people remarked that they made him look wiser and more mature. A full head of black hair accented his handsome, narrow face.

Whenever he could find time, Shinichi went fishing. The local river furnished plenty of crucian carp, and Shinichi seemed to have a hook that lured the fish to it. By the end of the day, Shinichi always claimed a substantial catch. To the surprise of nearby fishermen, the boy returned the fish he had caught to the water. Shinichi's reward was the act of fishing itself. He did not need to take home a full net to be happy. Masakichi had taught that not every activity needed to be for profit. Shinichi and his siblings learned this lesson well.

Not only could Shinichi throw out a fishing line, he could throw a baseball, too. He played for the commercial school team, usually pitching. At home he practiced heaving stones to catch cicadas. His aim was good, but that talent also led him into trouble.

Once, while attending commercial school, Shinichi was invited on a special expedition. The group of travelers were looking for biological research specimens. After docking at the island of Chishima, the members of the expedition left the ship for a walk along the beach of Cape Kokutan. Within minutes, one of the professors stopped, gazing up at a cliff.

"Oh, I wish I had some of that moss up there," Professor Emoto said.

Shinichi raised a hand to shield his eyes from the sunlight. He could see the reddish-cobalt colored moss on the side of a steep cliff. It draped across the rocks like a blanket.

"I'll get you some," Shinichi declared, his voice full of confidence. "Lend me a scoop," he said. "One heavy enough to toss up there."

The members of the expedition party exchanged puzzled looks. Surely Shinichi was joking. But one of the boys extended a small metal scoop used for digging. Shinichi positioned himself, gripping the scoop tightly. "Heavens!" he thought suddenly, realizing the throw was much more difficult then he had thought. He wished he could take back his words. But everyone was watching. He could not turn back now. With a mighty heave, Shin sent the scoop flying toward the cliff. The sound of the missile was muffled by the thick moss. Shinichi and the party waited, but the scoop did not return. It was caught firmly in the moss.

Shinichi felt his stomach turn flipflops. Inside, he knew his intention had not been to merely gather moss for the professor. He had wanted to impress those in the expedition. He hung his head in shame. The worst thing a Japanese child could do was bring dishonor to his family by displaying vanity. He had done just that!

Shinichi wished he could take his words back—and that he had never thrown that scoop. But now it was too late. He spotted a rock nearby, a stone as big as his fist. He ran to it and grabbed it, clutching it firmly. "Watch out! The scoop will fall down when I hit the handle," he announced. With as much anger as aim, the boy hurled the rock skyward towards the cliff. Clang! The stone hit the handle of the scoop. The metal instrument came crashing to the ground, moss wrapped all around it.

Astonished, Professor Emoto stared at Shinichi. Members of the expedition party broke into applause. Shinichi gazed at the moss-covered scoop on the ground. In that moment, Shinichi promised in his heart never to do such a foolish thing again.

Chapter Two

Big Decisions

"First character, then ability."

Sixteen-year-old Shinichi Suzuki stared up at the words on the tablet hanging in the main lecture room of Nagoya Commercial School. His teacher's lecture drifted into the distance. "First character, then ability."

So much of what his father said meant the same thing. The best of politicians, of businessmen, of artists, could only truly succeed if they were good people to begin with. Whatever they achieved of quality depended on what they were inside.

A tap on Shinichi's shoulder brought him back to reality. He turned to face a classmate who whispered an invitation to play baseball after the lecture. Shinichi knew he had studying to do—there was a major economics exam the next day. Nonetheless, the boy nodded agreement to the invitation. Throwing a ball was always more fun than reading a book.

While his teachers shook their heads at Shinichi's mediocre test scores and rushed term papers, his class-mates hailed him as their leader. Each year, they elected him as their class president. Whether it was his talents on the baseball diamond, his handsome face and quick smile, or his willingness to listen to their problems, Shinichi Suzuki was the most popular boy in his class.

Students from the Nagoya Commercial School often visited factories and businesses in the city. As the leader of his class, Shinichi took charge of meeting the hosting officials. The boy was good with strangers, practicing the behavior skills emphasized by his father: *Always greet a stranger with 'How do you do?,' A bow before your elders will make a good impression, Words from a smiling mouth win friends, a frown chills the air.* Shinichi knew the family maxims well and displayed them with warmth and charm. By the time the visit was finished, Shinichi was often offered a job after his graduation by one of the company officials.

But Shinichi Suzuki gave little thought to his future. He always knew there would be work for him at his father's factory. That would come soon enough, the boy thought.

However, there were big changes taking place in Japan in the early 1900s. Fifteen-year old Emperor Meiji had been placed into power after a restorative coup ousted Emporer Tokugawa—the last of the *shogun* rulers in Japan. The reign, or "enlightened rule" of Emporer Meiji, marked the beginning of Japan's formation into a modern state and the downfall of the old feudal government. Along with political reforms, such as the creation of a constitutional government, Emporer Meiji instituted reforms in education. He established a compulsory six-year education system for Japanese children and increased the country's literacy rate to ninety-eight percent by 1912.

Emporer Meiji's government also allowed the growth of Christianity in Japan, and he supported industrial reforms that changed Japan from a farming nation into a major industrial empire. Meiji sent representatives to many other countries to bring back new and better ideas for improving Japan. Exports increased significantly.

Masakichi Suzuki cheerfully welcomed the new reforms and government officials visited his successful factory. The violin maker wanted to know the latest and best ways of manufacturing his product and marketing it. Soon the violins were pouring out of the Suzuki factory, with production jumping from forty to 400 instruments daily in a period of less that five years.

"There is much for each of you to do," the father told his sons, "but you must learn the new ways, for I cannot learn all there is." Even while his factory turned out quality instruments with speed, Masakichi Suzuki continued to make his own violins by hand.

As Shinichi entered his senior year at the Nagoya Commercial School, his plans after graduation were still uncertain. Yet he was sure of one thing: He wanted to get the best grades he could. He was tired of getting mediocre marks. But one incident nearly ruined all his hard work.

It happened when Shinichi and his senior classmates were taking their final exams. One student noticed another student cheating and loudly announced the fact to the teacher. The cheating student was sent from the room, leaving the rest of the students in an uproar. Once the exam was over, many of the other students waited for the informant to leave the classroom. When he did, they jumped him and gave him a "sound thrashing." Shinichi was still in the classroom, packing his books. But as class president, he was sent for and made his way to the faculty room.

"What is the meaning of this outrageous attack?" one teacher demanded. "Were you aware of it?"

"I was," Shinichi lied. "I struck him too."

"What! Who are the students that struck him?"

"All the members of the class, sir."

"And you think you did right, do you?"

"I do not, sir. I think it was wrong to cheat, but it was extremely unfriendly to report him. Please punish us."

Shinichi returned to the room where his classmates were waiting. He knew they expected leadership from him, and so he made a rash request.

"What we did we had to do out of friendship. If you all agree, I'd like to say it was sanctioned by all of us. And this year I want everyone to accept a failure on the examination."

It was a bold suggestion. Yet when the vote was taken, all agreed, even those who had not taken part in the assault. One by one, the students were called into the faculty room and questioned.

Shinichi hated telling his father that he would fail his senior year, but it had to be done. Hanging his head, Shinichi asked his father to put him through school still another year. Masakichi Suzuki offered a noble smile. "Well, it can't be helped, can it?" he said simply.

Shinichi remembered an earlier incident at the violin factory, when the chief of the export department had caught him punching the keys of an English typewriter.

"Master Shinichi, you mustn't type without paper in the machine," the chief warned.

"Oh, but I'm not really punching the keys down," Shinichi said.

The chief turned and left the room. Shinichi shook his head, angry and ashamed at lying.

He left the factory, disgusted with himself. Trying to divert his attention, Shinichi went into a book store, where he came upon a small, worn book. As the boy flipped open Tolstoy's *Diary*, his gaze fell upon the words: "To deceive oneself is worse than to deceive others."

Shinichi had lied both about the typewriter and the examination. He knew there was much to do to improve his own character. As he looked into his father's understanding face, the boy felt even more love and respect than ever.

When Shinichi arrived at the school the next morning, there was a notice on the bulletin board. Twenty students would be punished for the examination incident, ten with an indefinite suspension and ten with a reprimand. Shinichi Suzuki's name headed the list of those being indefinitely suspended.

"It's not fair!" one student called out, looking over Shinichi's shoulder. "You weren't even there, Shinichi."

"I hit him and I'm not on either list," offered another boy.

Students mumbled and grumbled throughout the day. On the following morning not one member of the 1,700 students at Nagoya Commercial School showed up for classes. It was a full-fledged sympathy strike.

Another day went by, and still no students went to school. Then another. It was a week before each student received a summons to report to the school auditorium. The principal, Yoshiki Nishimura, stood on the stage. The man was one of Shinichi's biggest heroes, and the boy knew how difficult it was for him to be there. He had created the motto, "First character, then ability." Now the man spoke with tears in his eyes, announcing that all would be forgotten and that the exams would be given again.

Usually, there were a few seniors who failed. Not in the class of 1916. Everyone passed and graduated.

Looking back on this period of his life, Shinichi said, "I consider that seventeen was the age at which my foundations were laid." He had begun to study Zen Buddhism and was greatly impressed by the priest Dogan. In his book of meditations called *Shushogi,* Dogan wrote: "It is the great Buddha Karma that illuminates life and lightens death: If the Buddha is in life and death, there is no life and death . . ." Shinichi studied with his mother's uncle, a Zen master named Fuzan Asano. Zen Buddhism introduced Shinichi to the relationships between reason, memory, and experience. As with Tolstoy's *Diary,* Shinichi was then beginning to understand morality and his responsibility to his life's purpose.

It was about this same time that a new machine entered the Suzuki home. It was not exactly new, but rather an older gramophone. Most people were buying modern electric models. The gramophone had to be wound by hand and had a horn as a loudspeaker, big enough for a child's head to fit inside.

To Shinichi Suzuki, the violin had only been a toy. All his life he had heard others play, family and friends, from tortured scratching to smooth flowing melodies. Yet, now that the household owned a gramophone, Shinichi had an urge to own a record. His budget could afford only one, and he decided to purchase Schubert's "Ave Maria." Mischa Elman was the violinist.

After cranking the machine, Shinichi slipped the record on. From the first note he heard, he was plunged into a dream. The sound of the violin was so sweet, so pure and perfect. The tone of the melody touched something deep inside Shinichi, and his spirits soared. Such beauty from a violin? It seemed impossible! Yet it was true.

Soon Shinichi brought a violin home from the factory. He listened to Mischa Elman play a Haydn minuet. Again, the music wrapped around Shinichi's soul. The boy carefully listened to the selection again. This time, he moved the bow across the strings of his own violin. He did it several times. The sound was harsh, hardly close to a recognizable imitation.

In the days that followed, Shinichi practiced the piece again and again. Slowly, the notes became more crisp, more familiar. The boy felt good with the violin in his hands, and the music stirred a love and warmth within. Something new and wonderful had entered the life of Shinichi Suzuki. He had no idea how the violin would play a part in his future, but Shinichi knew it would.

Chapter Three

New Directions

Soon after Shinichi's graduation from Nagoya Commercial School, the Suzuki family made a move. Living next door to the violin factory had its advantages, but Masakichi Suzuki knew he spent far too much time at his place of business. The new family home was only seventeen minutes away from the factory, yet it was far enough to make less frequent trips.

As a member of the Suzuki family, Shinichi was entitled to special privileges working at the factory. Whereas the general work force arrived at seven each morning, Suzuki family members could arrive at nine o'clock. After all, they were management.

"That's foolish!" Shinichi declared. "If I work at the violin factory, I arrive with the other workers."

It hardly posed a major hardship. While a student, Shinichi had always gotten up at five o'clock anyway so that he could wake his younger brothers and sisters and take them for a walk to Tsurni Park before breakfast. The seventeen minute walk to the violin factory was brisk and healthy. The normal workday ran until five in the afternoon, when Shinichi walked home.

"Shinichi's coming!" One of the neighborhood children was always ready to inform other boys and girls in the area. They loved jumping into his arms and hugging his legs. Sometimes they toppled him, then scrambled all over his thin, lanky frame. It was impossible to tell who enjoyed the nightly routine more—Shinichi or his four and five-year-old friends.

Often Shinichi brought his neighborhood friends into his home where they could play with his younger brothers and sisters. The sounds of children laughing delighted him. Children trusted everyone and had no doubts. They knew how to love and knew no hate. They were full of life. Shinichi loved being with them; he loved being one of them.

The evening hours were spent at supper, sharing quiet conversation. But soon Shinichi excused himself and hurried to his room. The violin was now an important part of each day. Hours slipped swiftly by as Shinichi drew his bow smoothly across the strings of his instrument. He loved buying new records, then imitating each one himself. His playing had become clear, crisp, and warm. Yet Shinichi certainly did not consider himself a violinist. He was starting to understand the nature of art. He knew that art, true art, reached more than the mind or intellect. Art, whether it be musical art, visual art, or performing art—touched the heart and soul of the performer, reaching out to an audience of appreciators.

Sometimes Shinichi felt guilty about how wonderful his life was. He was surrounded by people he loved. He enjoyed his job at the violin factory. His violin brought him joy and pleasure. There was much to be thankful for.

When family friends invited Shinichi on a cruise, he accepted. Both the Marquis Tokugawa and Miss Nobu Koda were skilled musicians. They were amazed when they first heard Shinichi play his violin.

"You've taught yourself that?" the Marquis Tokugawa asked, obviously impressed with what he had heard.

"Why don't you study music instead of working at the violin factory?" Miss Koda asked.

Little more was said about the matter. Shinichi was not ready to think about studying music professionally. Life was going just fine for him as it was.

But when the Marquis Tokugawa came to visit Masakichi Suzuki and suggested his son take music lessons, the violin maker listened intently. The Marquis Tokugawa knew much about music. If he thought Shinichi had talent, it had to be true. The decision was left to Shinichi.

Shinichi hesitated at making any major changes in his life. After all, things were going very well as they were. Yet if so many people thought he should explore his possible musical talent, who was he to refuse the opportunity? The violin factory would be there if the music lessons failed to uncover any artistic ability within him.

Shinichi Suzuki traveled to Tokyo to study with Ko Ando, Miss Koda's younger sister. Her assignment was to teach Shinichi the rudiments of the violin. Professor Ryutaro Hirota gave him private lessons in music theory, while Professor H. Tanabe taught him acoustics. Shinichi was given a room in Marquis Tokugawa's mansion. Once a week, Shinichi worked with Ko Ando, and he practiced for hours every day. In the evenings he shared visits with those who came to see his host. The Marquis Tokugawa had a wide assortment of friends, many of them scholars and teachers. One night, it might be Kotoji Satsuda, the famed genius of words and language. The next night it could be the great physicist Torahiku Terada. The topics discussed ranged from religion to politics with business thrown in too.

"It is a kind of night school," Shinichi wrote home. "But there are no written examinations."

There were no "written examinations" from Mrs. Ando either—only the weekly lessons and daily practices. Shinichi was happy with his progress. After several months Mrs. Ando suggested he enroll at the music academy in Ueno. Not only could he study the violin and music, he could take other courses too. Shinichi agreed, and he prepared to take the entrance examination at Ueno.

"You might wish to hear the graduation recital," Mrs. Ando suggested.

That sounded like a good idea to Shinichi. He would be able to hear what he might sound like after completing his studies at Ueno. As Shinichi entered the Ueno concert hall on recital night, an excited chill raced through his body. He was sure he was in for a night of wonderful music.

Shinichi could not have been more mistaken. From the opening selection until the final number, he squirmed in his seat. The sounds from the stage were awful. He hurried to talk to Mrs. Ando the next day.

"I heard the graduation recital last night," Shinichi said. "If that's the best I can do after studying at Ueno, I do not want to take the entrance examination. I would rather go on studying with you, if I may."

Mrs. Ando smiled. "All right, if that's what you prefer. But you'll have to work hard."

Shinichi did exactly that, throwing all his energy into improving his skills with the violin. Even when the Marquis Tokugawa invited Shinichi to travel around the world with him for a year, the dedicated student refused. There was so much to learn; Shinichi was only beginning.

But a Japanese son does not refuse his father. Masakichi Suzuki thought the journey would be a perfect trip for Shinichi. "You can probably make the trip for 150,000 yen," the elder Suzuki declared. "Take the trip. Whatever money you have left over, you can spend studying the violin in Germany. I am informed they have fine teachers there." The discussion was over. In autumn of 1920,

Shinichi boarded the luxury liner *Hakone Maru.*

For many weeks, Shinichi played the role of a sightseer. This was not the Marquis Tokugawa's first trip around the world, and he proved an excellent guide. But by the time they reached Marseilles, France, where the Marquis had a suite of rooms, Shinichi was eager to continue his studies with the violin. He headed to Berlin.

Mrs. Ando offered to provide an introduction to several violin teachers she knew in Berlin, but Shinichi refused. At twenty-two, he felt old enough to find his own teacher.

After getting a hotel room, Shinichi embarked on an unusual mission. Every day he went to different concerts in the city. Some featured famous performers; others focused on unknown beginners. Shinichi listened closely. He knew what he wanted. Weeks slipped into months. Not finding what he was looking for in Berlin, Shinichi made plans to go to Vienna. But before he left, he went to hear the Klingler Quartet play at the Sing Academy. They had a fine reputation.

As the Klingler Quartet began playing, Shinichi leaned forward in his seat. And then, an amazing thing happened. As the group played Mozart's *Clarinet Quintet in A Major,* Shinichi closed his eyes and felt as if the music had been composed for him, that the group was playing for him alone. Love, truth, goodness, and beauty were perfectly blended and joined in harmony. Within the music Shinichi heard a message from Mozart to further the happiness of all people. Like the message in Tolstoy's *Diary*, Mozart's music fostered Shinichi's belief that the "life force itself . . . is the whole basis of man's being."

Since he could not write German, Shinichi wrote a note in English to Professor Karl Klingler, the quartet's leader and violinist, saying, "Please take me as your pupil."

Once his note was sent, Shinichi waited. When he told his Japanese friends what he had done, they were shocked.

"Klingler takes no private students," a young man in Shinichi's hotel said.

"You are wasting your time hoping," added another friend. "He probably tossed your note aside the moment he read it."

But before Shinichi had a chance to pack his bags for Vienna, a message arrived from Klingler. It was one word—the very word Shinichi Suzuki wanted to receive. "Come," it read. This simple command was to begin Shinichi's eight-year stay in Germany to study violin.

Shinichi had no idea where Professor Klingler lived, and he had to ask strangers for directions. When the door opened, Shinichi was greeted by a handsome man of about forty.

"You play so well," Shinichi gushed, fumbling with his violin case. "Every note was—"

Professor Klingler smiled, but raised his hand to silence his nervous visitor. "It matters little as to how I play. What concerns me now is how YOU play."

Shinichi trailed after his host, entering a large room. There was a small podium and Klingler extended his hand for his guest to climb on it. "I would like to hear the Rode *Concerto*," the professor requested.

Quickly Shinichi readied himself with his instrument. He knew he would hear little of what he was playing because his heart was beating so loudly. His fingers fumbled a bit with the bow. He could feel a cool sweat covering his body. Finally, as composed as he could make himself, he began.

Professor Klingler closed his eyes, concentrating on each note. His right hand moved on the arm of the chair. No, he was not counting time. Shinichi wondered what he thought.

Suddenly a nasty scratching sound infected the air. A mistake. A glaring error. Shinichi's first thought was to make a quick escape, not wanting to listen to the scolding that was sure to follow. But instead, he began the passage again, this time gliding through the music without a flaw. Still, the mistake had been made. "This is the end," Shinichi thought.

Finished, the young violinist stood at the podium. He wanted to make a quick exit but his feet felt like heavy rocks. His head hung in shame.

Professor Klingler rose to his feet. "When can you come again?" he asked.

Shinichi shook his head in disbelief. It seemed impossible. This great violinist—this teacher who did not accept private students—had just asked him to return. Could it be a dream? No, the words echoed in Shinichi's head. "When can you come again?" Shinichi repeated these words again and again all the way back to his hotel room.

Chapter Four

Understanding Art

Before studying with Professor Klingler, Shinichi Suzuki had paid little attention to the composers of musical selections. It was the music that was important. Who cared about the life of the composer?

Professor Klingler cared, there was no doubt about that. Before one note of any selection was played, the instructor shared the story behind the composition.

"Could Handel have written the *Messiah* without his own personal spiritual passion?" the professor asked. "We can never hope to play a selection as its creator intended unless we know what force compelled him to do so. Mozart, Beethoven, Brahms—each had something happening inside that had to come out in music."

Only after Professor Klingler had told Shinichi the story behind a piece of music, would he raise his bow and play. Shinichi listened, remembering how often he had heard the selection—and yet realizing that he had never truly heard it before. One had to understand the composer to understand his art. Only then was it time to attempt playing the composition. The professor played without error, his body poised and graceful, the music warm and sensitive.

Then it was Shinichi's turn to play. At first, he felt clumsy, ashamed at his own efforts. He wanted to impress his teacher, to make the professor gasp with delight. Yet it did not happen. Patiently Professor Klingler corrected Shinichi's mistakes, whether they be in time or note. The lessons often lasted two hours or more. Klinger assigned several pieces for each lesson, and Shinichi presented each one.

Shinichi moved from his hotel into a boarding house. His landlord was an elderly woman with a live-in maid. Both women were hard of hearing, allowing Shinichi to practice any time of the night or day. Dr. Michaelis, a friend of his father's, kept an eye on Shinichi, inviting him to dinner often and making sure he had no problems. It was a good relationship, and Shinichi was sorry when Dr. Michaelis announced he was moving to the United States.

"I shall not leave you alone here in Berlin, however," the kind doctor declared. "I have a good friend who has agreed to act as your guardian while you are studying here. He is quite a well-known scientist. His name is Albert Einstein."

Shinichi had heard of Albert Einstein. People called him a great thinker and mathematician.

Shinichi soon discovered that Dr. Einstein was not only a scientist and mathematician, he was a musician as well—a violinist, of all things! The man carried his violin everywhere. At dinner parties, he was always willing to lift a bow and share his talents. Shinichi admired his guardian's deft finger movements, his beautifully delicate tone. Just like his teacher, Professor Klingler, Dr. Einstein made playing the violin look so easy.

But Dr. Einstein was as big a fan of Shinichi as he was of the talented doctor. Once, at a dinner party, Shinichi was encouraged to play a selection. He chose a concerto by the German composer Max Bruch. Afterwards, while the guests sipped their tea, an elderly woman shook her head.

"I really can't understand it," the lady said to those around her. "This young man is Japanese, having grown up in a totally different environment than ours. Yet in spite of that, his performance clearly expressed to me the Germaness of Bruch. Tell me, is such a thing possible?" Shinichi was dumbfounded.

Dr. Einstein paused, tea cup in hand, and smiled at the woman who was old enough to be his mother. "People are all the same, madame," he said softly and respectfully.

Shinichi was tremendously moved by the observation. It was such a simple truth. He was grateful to be studying with Professor Klingler, who recognized that it was so important to understand and know the composer before playing his music. Notes were much more than marks on paper. They were imprints of a creator's heart and soul. Yes, that was true art—when a person could reach deep within and create in a way that shared emotion and sensitivity with another person, even a total stranger.

Shinichi's relationship with Dr. Einstein deepened. Close friends supplied the doctor with concert tickets to hear the best performers who came to Berlin. "I have tickets," Dr. Einstein would say to Shinichi on the telephone. "Let's go."

Shinichi never turned down an invitation. The performance might not be as good as he hoped, but an evening spent with Dr. Einstein was never wasted time. The man seemed to know everyone, and everyone he knew was the best in their field. The conversations were sparkling, ideas popping back and forth like tennis balls on a court. Even when he knew nothing about the topic, Shinichi was always included and encouraged to ask questions. His mind took notes, building and growing, absorbing new ways of thinking. Harmony was not only a musical term. Shinichi realized it was a way of living, willingly sharing and growing in every way.

Shinichi's respect for his teacher, Professor Klingler, grew greater every day. His violin playing was improving. Professor Klingler moved the lessons from concertos and sonatas to chamber music. The teacher was a master of the medium, and Shinichi became a devoted fan. Chamber music is music composed and intended for a small audience, maybe fewer than ten people. Shinichi had no intention of being a public performer, but he knew if he ever did, he would like the intimacy of chamber music.

Shinichi wrote home to his family:

> It is not merely the music that is helping me to grow here in Berlin, although Professor Klingler is truly an outstanding teacher. He has helped me to know that a truly fine violinist is one who understands the nature of art before doing anything with his hands and body. Beyond the lessons it is the conversations. Dr. Michaelis and his friends opened my thinking to so many new ideas. Dr. Einstein has made the opening even larger. This is a grand place to be!

One night Shinichi accompanied Dr. Einstein to a piano concert at the home of a man named Dr. Franke. One young lady in the audience caught his eye with her appearance and poise. After the concert, Shinichi asked Waltraud Prange if he could walk her home. The next day, he met her family—mother, brother and sister—who all were musicians. Waltraud played piano and had a lovely voice. Her father had passed away.

Waltraud and Shinichi began going to dinner and attending concerts together. He loved hearing her sing, and she loved hearing him play. They loved being together, even when doing nothing. Her family received Shinichi well, and often, Shinichi would join them in their family concerts at home. Before long the couple became engaged.

They were married in Berlin on February 28, 1928. Shinichi had become a Catholic while living in Germany, and the wedding took place at the church where Waltraud was a soloist. The couple lived in Berlin for the next four months until Shinichi received a telegram that his mother was ill. Then, he and Waltraud left by train immediately.

Chapter Five

Discovery

Shinichi Suzuki found a different Japan in 1928 than the one he had left eight years before. Emporer Meiji had died sixteen years earlier, and now his grandson, Hirohito, was the new ruler. The country had become an industrial giant, competing against other nations around the world for countless products. The city of Nagoya was constantly growing. Masakichi Suzuki's violin factory was producing at an amazing rate of 500 instruments a day, and the finest musicians acclaimed his violins as "the best in the world."

If Shinichi had worried at all about the reception his wife might receive because she was from another culture and country, he worried for nothing. Shinichi's family and friends warmly welcomed Waltraud. Wherever the couple went, she was invited to sing. Waltraud had the Bechstein piano her mother had given her as a wedding present shipped to Japan.

"They seem to have forgotten I am a musician too," Shinichi teased. But there was only pride in his voice. He enjoyed listening to his wife perform more than anyone else.

After the newlyweds had been in Nagoya for almost a year, Shinichi's mother passed away.

There was much to do at the violin factory. In 1930, the Suzuki Violin Seizo Company was founded, a stream-lined version of the old manufacturing operation. The company soon became the largest violin-making com-pany in Japan. As a Suzuki family member, Shinichi was still considered a part of the management level. Yet he still enjoyed talking to the workers, remembering those times when he listened to the stories and ran to get the rice cake when the storyteller requested it.

But Shinichi Suzuki felt most comfortable with a violin in his hand, the bow gliding across the strings, the music of Mozart or Strauss filling the air. He was delight-fully surprised to discover that he was not the only family member drawn to music. Two of his brothers played the violin too, and another played the cello. With little effort, Shinichi convinced his brothers that they should practice together. Once they did, it was clear that the quality of their playing deserved greater exposure. The Suzuki String Quartet was born.

Invitations flowed in for the Suzuki String Quartet. Shinichi preferred playing in private homes, at dinner parties or in small settings, where the music could be intimate and personal. The four sons enjoyed performing for their father at home too.

Shinichi Suzuki not only enjoyed playing the violin, he enjoyed teaching it to others. Soon he was president of the Teioku Music School. Then he founded the Tokyo String Orchestra. He loved finding others who enjoyed music as much as he did. It was even more exciting introducing quality music to new listeners. It was not easy juggling his busy schedule, but he always seemed to find time to instruct another pupil.

One student, Toshiya Eto, posed a special problem. It was not that Toshiya did not want to learn to play—he did, and so did his father. "He will work hard for you," the man promised. "I will see that he practices as much as you say." Shinichi Suzuki nodded. The offer was probably true.

Toshiya Eto was only four years old. Shinichi had no experience teaching a child so young. Was it possible to do? The question hounded him morning to night.

Then, while Shinichi and his brothers were practicing together, the answer came "like a flash of light in a dark night." All Japanese children have learned to speak Japanese. They speak it easily and fluently. How? They were trained in their homes, with their parents, just like other children in countries around the world learn their languages. If young Japanese children could be taught their native language, considered to be very difficult, why could they not be taught other things? If a child could not do arithmetic, people considered his intelligence low.

Suzuki disagreed. It has nothing to do with intelligence, Suzuki reasoned, but rather with the training. The more he pondered the thought, the more convinced he was that it was true.

"I will be honored to work with your son," Suzuki told the father of Toshiya Eto. "Let us begin at once."

When word got out that Shinichi Suzuki was teaching very young students, parents came knocking at his door. He would always emphasize that they, the mother and father, would have to play an active role in the child's learning process. It had to be a team effort.

When an opportunity came to teach at the Imperial Conservatory in Tokyo, Suzuki could not refuse. The school maintained a fine reputation of training young musicians. It was not easy leaving his family in Nagoya, but Shinichi and Waltraud promised to return often. Surprisingly enough, some of the families of his students also moved to Tokyo.

"Music has changed our lives," said the parents of another young student. "We would follow Shinichi Suzuki anywhere as long as he would teach our son."

During the 1930s, Shinichi thrived on teaching. He also formulated his theory to nurture musical ability in young people. It demanded parent involvement, preferably as early as possible. It was important that a baby enjoy music as early as possible in the home. Singing, even off-key, by members of the family was encouraged. Records were to be played, and instruments could be

Dr. Suzuki met acclaimed scientist and fellow musician Albert Einstein in Germany.
(Courtesy of the Library of Congress.)

Dr. Suzuki met President Jimmy Carter at Kennedy Center in Washington, D. C. during the 1978 International Talent Education Tour. *(Courtesy of the Jimmy Carter Library.)*

Dr. Suzuki and a student, 1976. *(Photograph © Arthur Montzka.)*

Dr. Suzuki, 1976. *(Photograph © Arthur Montzka.)*

Dr. and Mrs. Shinichi Suzuki, 1978. *(Photograph © Arthur Montzka.)*

After hearing a concert performed by Dr. Suzuki's students, renowned cellist Pablo Casals (far left) stated "perhaps it is music that will save the world." *(Courtesy of the Library of Congress)*

practiced by others in the home. A child would therefore want to share in the musical experience.

The simple "Twinkle, Twinkle, Little Star" seemed an appropriate selection for young musician to begin with. Sheet music or note memorization was not possible at this young age. Learning to read music would come later. But even the youngest child could listen to music and learn to make the sounds on an instrument. Once a student learned one selection, new music would be introduced following the same pattern of learning. Listening to records every day was essential. Hearing a selection again and again would lead to successful imitation.

"But does the child not become just a machine?" someone asked. Shinichi shook his head. "The child will develop a strong musical sense and be able to perform music at a superior level. Character will be developed as well. One must be endowed with all three together. A true artist is a person with beautiful and fine feelings, thoughts and actions. This is the message I hand down to my students."

Suzuki's message spread. When he was not teaching students at the Imperial Conservatory, he was teaching children in his home or organizing recitals and performances. Each one helped to give the pupils confidence. At the same time, the sights and sounds of young people playing brought new joy to their parents and friends.

Perhaps none of Suzuki's students received as much attention as his young pupil, Koji Toyoda. At only three years old, the boy made his public debut at the Nihon Seinenkan in Tokyo. With his father accompanying him on the guitar, Koji played Dvorák's "Humoresque" on his one-sixteenth size violin. When he finished, the boy took a bow to the waves of applause. The next day, his picture appeared in all the Tokyo newspapers. The headlines read "A Genius Appears" and "Brilliant." As his teacher read the articles to him the next day, Koji wiggled and squirmed. "May we get to the practice time?" the three-year-old asked politely. Shinichi Suzuki nodded and smiled. Yes, to the music. That was what it was all about.

Suzuki came to call his learning program Talent Education. He was convinced that all children, if properly trained, had talent that could enrich their lives and the lives of those around them. Koji and others might be labeled "geniuses," but they were not born as such. His talent had been fostered. He had been brought up listening to records every day. It was no strain for him to practice well. The child had played "Humoresque" so well because he had listened to it and practiced it over and over.

The largest challenge yet of Shinichi's philosophy occured in 1937. When five-year lod Teiichi Tanaka arrived to meet Shinichi Suzuki, an amazing bond was formed. The boy was blind, the victim of a disease that required both eyes to be removed. His father, an oil painter, posed an unusual challenge.

"My wife and I want to give our son a light in the darkness," Mr. Tanaka told Suzuki. "A light that will shine throughout his life. We were thinking of music, and I came to ask you to accept him as one of your violin students."

Suzuki looked down at the small boy standing before him. The child would never see a sunrise or a flower. Tears welled in the music master's eyes. Of course he wanted to say yes, but how could the boy learn to play? Was it fair for Suzuki to accept him out of sympathy or pity?

"Let me think about it," Suzuki answered. "Please return in one week."

That night Suzuki sat in his study. Images of young Teiichi Tanaka kept returning to him. Suddenly, the music master rose to his feet. He turned off the light. Carefully, Suzuki felt his way to the table where he had put his violin. He felt the case with his hands and opened it. He removed the instrument. Everything took longer in the dark, yet it was possible. Positioning the violin and bow, Suzuki began to play. In the dark, he became more aware of the tip of the bow, the strings, the bridge, and his finger positions. In fact, the sense of touch was even more sensitive in the dark, and the lack of light did not affect his playing at all.

"Yes, I will make little Teiichi see the violin, strings, and bow," Suzuki told himself. "He doesn't need physical eyes if I can teach him to use his spiritual ones."

The task was not easy. Suzuki and Teiichi spent weeks merely feeling the bow, moving it right and left, up and down. The procedure, so simple for a person with sight, proved a major chore for a blind five year old. But finally, he succeeded. With his parents' help and Suzuki's patience, Teiichi was able to hold the violin and bow correctly. But when he would practice the exercise of lifting the bow to the violin five times in a row, he missed once each time.

"Well, that was a miss," Suzuki would say cheerfully. "Let's start all over again, and now you will make it five times continuously. You can do it. You can do it."

The process moved slowly and weeks turned into months. But Teiichi would not give up—and neither would his teacher. Once the bow and tip became "visible" to the boy's imagination, he started to play songs on the violin. One year after he started working with Suzuki, six-year old Teiichi Tanaka played at Hibiya Hall in Tokyo. The bow moved gracefully across the strings as he performed the Seitz *Concerto*. Many people wept as they listened, including his proud music teacher. The applause shook the building, while some people dabbed at their eyes with their handkerchiefs. Teiichi bowed, his violin in one hand and his bow in the other.

While Shinichi Suzuki surrounded himself with children and heard the sounds of their instruments, major changes were taking place at high levels of the Japanese government. Military leaders took control, convincing the people that Emperor Hirohito was a god, and that the world should be united by his divine rule. Newspapers and radio programs told the people that they must support the military leaders who represented the emperor. Some influential people resisted and argued. These people were killed, many by army officers. The constant stream of propaganda convinced the Japanese people that it was their destiny to control the world.

While Germany, led by Adolph Hitler, invaded European countries, Japan took their military forces into Asia. The United States and several other countries protested by stopping the supply of goods sent to Japan. War clouds were forming.

Chapter Six

Sounds of War

United States President Franklin D. Roosevelt called December 7, 1941, "a date that will live in infamy." In the early morning hours, Japanese aircraft bombed American navy installations at Pearl Harbor, Hawaii. The United States officially declared war on Japan the next day. Japan became an ally of Germany and Italy. The world was in turmoil.

Shinichi Suzuki found his own life suddenly turned upside-down. In Nagoya, his father made the violin factory into a factory to produce seaplane floats. "If it is for the divine and honorable Emperor of Japan, then it must be done," said Masakichi Suzuki, trying to adjust to a new way of life and work. The sight of seaplane floats brought tears to his eyes; the eighty-three-year old man preferred to remember the days of making beautiful instruments.

Cypress wood was needed to build the seaplane floats

in Nagoya, but there was no easy way to bring it into the factory. Someone needed to go into the Kiso-Fukushima Mountains and bring the wood back. Otherwise, no work could be done.

Although air raids in Tokyo became more frequent, Shinichi's students would not leave the dangerous area. They were willing to risk their lives to keep up with their music. This worried their teacher. Shinichi was also concerned about his wife's safety. Although her homeland of Germany was a wartime ally of Japan, all foreigners were regarded with some suspicion. Two mountain resorts were set aside for Germans living in Japan, Karuizawa and Hakone. Since Shinichi and Waltraud had a cottage at Hakone, he encouraged her to go there where she would be safe.

"And what will you do?" Waltraud asked.

"I will try to get the cypress wood from Kiso-Fukushima," Shinichi answered.

Suzuki knew nothing about lumber, but he learned fast. Soon the lumber was being sawed in the Kiso-Fukushima factory and sent to the seaplane float factory in Nagoya.

Waltraud could not leave the German village at Hakone, and Shinichi could only visit his wife every two months. He longed for those times, but he knew he was needed back at Kiso-Fukushima. Although Shinichi missed Waltraud, he was glad she was in a safe place.

In Kiso-Fukushima, Shinichi boarded with a family named Doke. When Shinichi returned home from work at the lumber factory one night, he found unexpected guests. His sister was there with her two children. Like so many Japanese families, his sister Hina had lost her husband to the war. They had nowhere else to go. The Doke family took them in.

On one visit to Hakone, Waltraud greeted Shinichi with a surprise wrapped in tissue: an apple. Since Shinichi knew Waltraud was on strict rations, it was a very special gift. Yet he could not bring himself to eat it. Instead, he took the apple back to Kiso-Fukushima, where he divided it into quarters and gave it to his sister's two children.

As World War II continued, the living conditions worsened. No food was produced in or around Kiso-Fukushima, as it was surrounded by mountains and small valleys. The rations dwindled. Shinichi and the other workers ventured into the highlands where they searched the mountain streams. Finding algae along the rocks, they filled their sacks and brought it back to town. Once boiled, the algae formed a meager sustenance. It was not much, but it helped stave off hunger.

News of bombing raids in other Japanese cities reached the town. Kiso-Fukushima was tucked inland among the mountains, therefore no enemy airplanes struck the homes and factories. But reports of the deaths of loved ones arrived daily. On January 31, 1944, Shinichi mourned the death of his father, Masakichi Suzuki.

Day after day, the people of the town carried out their daily tasks. To keep spirits up, Shinichi played his violin each morning. The music graced the clear mountain air and helped the people forget how little they had to eat and how miserable they were. The working hours became longer, up to twelve and fourteen hours a day. Yet the people seemed happier working because it allowed them to focus on something other than their difficult lives.

Finally, word reached Kiso-Fukushime that the war was over. Japan had surrendered to the United States after the Americans had dropped atomic bombs on the Japanese cities of Hiroshima and Nagasaki. Emperor Hirohito spoke to the nation on the radio. The long struggle was over.

Shinichi, like everyone else, wondered what changes would be coming. Would the allied victors want to squeeze a deeper revenge on Japan? Would the suffering continue?

The Americans now governed Japan. General Douglas MacArthur established a seat of power in Tokyo. The Emperor was not overthrown, and a select group of Japanese leaders were installed to work with the Americans.

Over the next few months it became clear that the Americans did not intend to be severe victors. A few of the top Japanese military leaders were tried and sentenced to be executed. But there would not be extreme economic penalites placed on the Japanese people. It was time to return to the peaceful life that had been interrupted by the war.

Shinichi began wondering about the location of some

of his students. He was especially interested in locating Koji. He learned that both of young Koji's parents had died. This saddened him greatly and motivated him to work harder to find the young student. Koji may need someone to take care of him.

Shinichi began writing letters to see if he could locate his former student. It was easier than he thought. Within weeks, eleven-year-old Koji showed up at the Doke home with an uncle. The man was delighted to put his nephew in Shinichi's care.

It was clear that Koji needed a lot of work. The boy had been living with his uncle who ran a *sake* (a Japanese alcoholic beverage made from rice) bar, and he had developed many bad habits and poor manners. Shinichi, his sister, and her two children dedicated themselves to helping Koji better himself.

"Do not scold or lecture the boy," Shinichi told his sister and her children. "He will learn more by observing your good behavior."

Shinichi's advice proved wise. Thanks to their help, Koji improved quickly. He helped out when he could.

Shinichi Suzuki wanted to move on with his life. He had given three years to the factory in Kiso-Fukushima. He was eager to rejoin Waltraud. He was also anxious to get back to his music—and to share that love with others. When he received a letter from a former teaching colleague about starting a music school in Matsumoto, Shinichi responded immediately. But he had definite opinions about what he wanted to do in a new music school.

> I am not very interested in doing 'repair work' on people who can play already. I did enough of that in Tokyo. What I want to try is infant education. I have worked out a new method I want to teach to small children—not to turn out geniuses but through violin playing to extend the child's ability. I have been doing this research for many years. That is why I want to put all my efforts into this kind of education in the future. If my idea finds approval, I will help with teaching along these lines.

Shinichi waited. Within weeks the answer came. Yes, he had been given permission to open the Matsumoto Music School. This was exciting news.

In December of 1945, Shinichi left Kiso-Fukshima and headed to Matsumoto. Money and jobs were scarce in Japan after the war. When Waltraud was offered a job with the American Red Cross in Yokohama, she did not want to accept. Shinichi wanted her to turn down the offer too, but they had little choice. Until Shinichi became established in his new position, there would be no money coming in. Shinichi found a small place to stay in Matsumoto. As soon as the music school became successful, Shinichi planned to bring his wife to stay with him.

Once in Matsumoto, Shinichi Suzuki had little opportunity to promote his Talent Education Program. A victim of recurring stomach problems since he was a student in Germany, he became ill. Much of his ailments stemmed from his own neglect. His daily meals consisted of a rice dumpling or two in a potful of soup. Day after day he ate the same thing, and each day he grew weaker.

One day a teacher from the Matsumoto Music School stopped by. Misako Koike was shocked at what she found. Shinichi could not even stand up. He had to crawl across the floor. Miss Koike summoned a friend of hers who was a Chinese doctor. Mrs. Uehara was also stunned at Shinichi's condition. He appeared to be days away from death. With a change of diet and lots of rest, Shinichi would recover. He promised to do whatever Mrs. Uehara told him. The daily meal of rice gruel disappeared. In its place came pickled vegetables and unpolished rice. The new menu activated Shinichi's stomach, allowing him to consume more foods. Within a month, he was on his feet and walking.

Shinichi's sister Hina was a big help too. She came to help him with his recovery, bringing her two children and Koji. They took good care of their patient. Because Waltraud was the only family member making money, she could only visit on weekends.

One incident spurred Shinichi into action. It was a cold winter night, well below zero, when Hina returned from an errand. As she shook off the snow, she told of a tired soldier she had seen begging by the river.

"He is standing there shivering in this driving snow,

and nobody is putting any money in the box at his feet. I wanted to invite him in to sit in our warm room and give him some tea."

Shinichi looked surprised. "You merely wanted to?" he replied, his voice reflecting his disbelief at what she had said.

Hina looked down. "Yes," she answered.

In the next moment she was out the door and back on the street. Shinichi warmed the room more and located some cookies a friend had dropped by. About thirty minutes later, his sister returned with the white-clad, shivering, wounded soldier.

"This lady insisted—" the stranger began to explain.

"You are very welcome," said Shinichi. "Do come in."

The soldier responded quickly to the friendliness of his hosts. They treated him like a special guest. It was clear that he had not eaten in some time. Laughter, too, had become unfamiliar. For several minutes conversation flowed, the soldier warming to the friendliness of his hosts. Finally, he looked around.

"Why are you so kind to me?" the man asked.

"My sister happened to see you," Shinichi replied, "and insisted on inviting you in."

The soldier looked down. "It's the first time any one has . . . and today was so cold and miserable."

The soldier stayed for three hours, sharing his war experiences and stories about his family. In the last few months he had chosen to try and raise money for other wounded soldiers, those who were more injured than he was. As the soldier turned to leave, Shinichi put some money in his box.

"But you have been so kind already," the soldier responded.

"We brought you here and you have lost half a day's business," said Shinichi. "You are collecting money for others. You cannot refuse what we would give them."

Once the soldier was gone, Shinichi's sister turned to him. "You taught me an excellent lesson," she said. "If you want to do something, do it."

They were simple words, and yet there was so much truth in them. That night, and in the days that followed, Shinichi Suzuki pondered those words often. "If you want do to something, do it." There were so many people who thought, "I'd like to do this, or that." But how many people actually carried out their thoughts? No action followed the thought in many cases. Dreams and opportunities simply slipped away.

Shinichi Suzuki was convinced that he was just such a person. He was a thinker but not a doer. If he honestly believed in his Talent Education Program—that the very young child could learn anything by imitation and repetition—someone had to take action. Shinichi was that someone.

Chapter Seven

Thoughts into Action

Shinichi Suzuki carefully worked out his plan for teaching young children to develop their abilities. Much of his program depended on the child's environment, especially parental involvement. Without their support, little could be achieved; with their support, anything seemed possible.

In 1949, Suzuki took his program for child education to the leader of the Hongo Primary School in Matsumoto. That year, Mrs. Yano's class of forty students was the first to begin learning by his method. Each day, the students were given a few easy exercises. The same exercises were reviewed the next day before going on to new material. In this way, the students reached the same high standards as their classmates.

Mrs. Yano's students were between the ages of three and five. Following Suzuki's method of imitation and repetition, the youngsters practiced Japanese pronounciation, Chinese letters, calligraphy, expression, English conversation, drawing, and gymnastics. Numbers from one to ten were also included. The students responded eagerly and displayed skills beyond their teacher's and Suzuki's expectations.

A special feature of the program was *haiku*. A haiku is a three-lined Japanese poem that usually has a theme concerning nature. The boys and girls counted the syllables—five in the first line, seven in the second, and five in the third—and memorized the works of the poet Issa. Then they wrote their own haiku. They captured the seasons, animals, and sounds of the world they knew—and the world they imagined—in language. In strong and pure voices, the children shared their haikus aloud with each other.

By 1950, Suzuki was ready to teach his students to play the violin at the Matsumoto Music School. He never intended to make master musicians out of his students. Character was the goal, building virtue within each individual. By listening to music early in life, a young person would develop a good ear. Later, when a violin was presented, (children used smaller violins until they grew big enough to play a regular-sized instrument), boys and girls could copy music they had heard. From the simplest composition, usually "Twinkle, Twinkle Little Star," to a Bach "Gavotte," the children could perform with poise and skill. Suzuki called his special music program the *Saino Kyoiku Kenkyu-kai*, or the "Talent Education Institute."

In the classroom, students played both privately and in groups. Students felt special receiving individual attention from their instructor. "I did it!" a child would exclaim, having played for his teacher. "Now I can play with the others!" Playing with other students allowed the student to grow with the better players and help those not so talented to improve.

Not only did the students attend classes, but their parents were encouraged to come also. They listened, took notes, and went to the private lessons of their children. Many of them even took up the violin themselves. Clearly, if children were to benefit from this program, parents would need to be vital participants.

The music master's new teaching concepts quickly attracted attention in educational circles. Teachers from across Japan came to observe. Before long, visitors came from other countries too.

"I was most skeptical about your teaching strategy before I visited your school," wrote a traveling teacher from France. "But once I saw and heard what your little people were doing, I was amazed. Bravo, my friend. May your method spread throughout the world."

Suzuki's method did indeed spread. Families moved to Matsumoto so that their children could attend his institute. Class lists doubled and tripled. Most of the students attended for only two years. In 1952, 196 students graduated.

Not only were parents thrilled with what their children

could do with the violin, they were delighted at the way other areas of their lives were affected. Boys and girls improved in neatness; they were more cooperative at home; they were more careful about doing tasks, taking their time in reading and writing, and discussing topics with greater depth.

Suzuki emphasized constantly that his method would only be successful with the full cooperation of the parents.

> You must have records in the home, selections that the child will hear in the morning when he wakes, in the afternoon when he rests, and in the evening when he goes to bed. Eventually, that child will raise the violin and seek those same notes, those same sounds. The instrument may be thought a toy at first. Playing it may be a game. Letting the child have fun is the secret to good learning.

"It is a strange way to teach music," offered one critic.

But teaching music was not Suzuki's main goal. "I want to make good citizens, noble human beings," Suzuki explained. "If a child hears fine music, and learns to play it himself, he develops sensitivity, discipline and endurance. He gets a beautiful heart."

There was little doubt that Suzuki's own young students believed he had the most beautiful heart of all. Patient and caring, he was never one to shout or yell. When a selection did not go particularly well, the gentle music teacher simply said, "I would like to hear that piece again." Often the child was not sure whether he had played well and pleased his teacher or played poorly and disappointed Suzuki. The second time around was always improved, bringing an appreciative smile—and perhaps a piece of candy from the teacher's seemingly bottomless pockets.

The number of Suzuki followers grew. Not only did students crowd his classes, but teachers came to study him and his method. Once trained, they dispersed to take his techniques into classrooms of their own. Some applied his approach to other instruments, including the cello, piano, and flute.

Suzuki was always a fan of fine classical music. Bach, Handel, Mozart—he knew the major composers well who had endured throughout centuries. But the western world had played a major part in Japan's culture, especially since the end of World War II. The American occupation of the country had introduced their music and instruments to the Japanese. Suzuki enjoyed the sounds from across the sea and encouraged those who liked it to play it. Guitars fascinated him too.

Despite the success and rapid growth of his method, Suzuki was not satisfied with doing the same thing. He wanted to strengthen his program and make his students even more focused. Once they could play "Twinkle, Twinkle Little Star," he walked around his classroom swiftly, asking his pupils questions while they performed. They were simple questions, such as, "How many legs do you have?" or "How many eyes do you have?" It was important that the children could answer while playing, doing two things at once. Just as a person should be able to speak while performing another task, Suzuki believed a child should be able to play a violin while listening and responding to something else. Then, the music was truly learned.

"But shouldn't a true musician concentrate totally on the selection he is playing?" someone asked.

The ever-patient Suzuki smiled and responded:

> Our goal is not to prepare students for the concert hall. What we want is for children to have fun with music and their instruments, to play for their own pleasure, to grow inside as people. We know that Japanese is a challenging language. Yet it is second nature to speak our language while running a machine or washing clothing. The child who seeks a profession in music will do so later, in his own way and through his own direction.

Many of Suzuki's former students did exactly that. He was especially proud of Koji, whom he helped send to France for further study. The boy managed to win his way to study with Georges Enesco, one of the world's most renowned violinists. In less than six months, Koji graduated from the Paris Conservatory. "You have been both my teacher and like my own father," the young man wrote back to Suzuki. "Without music, my life would be empty."

Koji Toyoda was only one of Suzuki's students who pursued a career in music. Toshiya Eto, Takeji Kobayashi, Kenji Kobayashi, and Yoko Sato were among the other boys and girls who began with the Suzuki method and attained quick attention as promising professional violinists.

Chapter Eight

A Special Visit

In 1961, Pablo Casals, the grand maestro of strings, was coming to Tokyo. At sixty-three, Shinichi Suzuki was seldom capable of being surprised. He had lived long enough and had seen so many situations that he knew anything might happen. But when Pablo Casals accepted Suzuki's invitation to hear his young people play the violin and cello, the music teacher was thrilled.

To Shinichi Suzuki and much of the rest of the world, Pablo Casals was the greatest string musician alive. Performer, composer, and conductor, he was a living legend, especially on the cello. He had played before presidents, kings, and millions of people during his lifetime. Born in Spain in 1876, Casals was a world traveler, with residences in many places. At eighty-four years old, the famous string master had decided to make a home in Japan. Shinichi Suzuki sent a courtesy invitation to Casals to attend a concert of young instrumentalists in Tokyo. The chances of the elderly musician accepting were slim indeed, or at least, so Suzuki thought. Time had taken its toll on Casals, and he spent much time within the grounds of his home.

But then the answer came: "I would be delighted to hear such a concert. Of course, I know of your method. I believe that all of the world does."

Plans were made quickly with every detail checked and rechecked. At ten o'clock on the morning of April 16, 1961, 400 children assembled on the stage of Bunkyo Hall in Tokyo. Their ages ranged from five to twelve, an older group of musicians trained with the Suzuki method.

Outside Bunkyo Hall, a sizable crowd gathered to witness the arrival of the noted visitor. People chatted, shifting to get a better viewing position for Casals's arrival. The limousine carrying the musician and his wife arrived shortly before ten a.m. Out of respect for the elderly guest, the voices immediately lowered. Feet stopped moving too, although heads craned to see. Slowly Pablo Casals exited the car, his wife at his side, and they entered the hall. From the moment the maestro came in, the audience stood, their hands clapping, their faces a sea of smiles. But Casals directed his attention to the stage, grinning at the 400 little bodies holding their instruments. "Oh, oh . . ." the old man exclaimed, obviously moved by the sight of so many children. He lifted an arm in a friendly wave, and the clapping swelled as if he were conducting. Within moments the visitors were in their seats, their ears and eyes focused on the young performers on the stage. Bows raised and the concert began.

"Twinkle, twinkle, little star . . ."

The violins played in unison, with many variations. The strokes were lively and sure, the eyes of the players alert, filled with energy and innocence. The pairs of feet stood firmly in place with no shaking or awkward movements. The countless hours of practicing showed. The desire to please the audience was obvious.

The performance continued with Vivaldi's *Concerto in A Minor* and Bach's *Double Violin Concerto*. Casals's gaze did not leave the stage. "Oh, oh . . . ," he said often in a voice filled with emotion. Amazed at what he saw, the old man wept.

Sixteen of the young performers moved forward, carefully maneuvering their cellos, then seating themselves at the front of the stage. Taught by Yoshio Sato, a student of Casals, the small group first played Saint-Saens' *The Swan*. Then they performed Bach's *Bourree*. The selections were flawless, with the notes of each instrument blending with the others. Casals shook his head in ectasy, his emotions knowing no bounds. Clearly, no one in the hall was enjoying the concert more than this man.

No one except for Shinichi Suzuki. He was proud that his young performers were playing so well. Of course, they could not know the joy they were giving to their family members and friends in the audience, but especially to one man who had given his life to music.

When the performance ended, Suzuki made his way to Pablo Casals. With a deep bow, he started to thank his honored guest for attending. "You have brought us great honor by listening to the young people perform. I want you to know—"

Pablo Casals would hear no more. The man threw his arms around Suzuki and leaned his face on his shoulder. Once more he cried. Suzuki understood. He, too, had wept as he heard the young people play in the past.

"I want to see them, to thank them," Casals said. Suzuki led the maestro and his wife to the stage. With smiles and gentle pats on shoulders, the couple mingled with the performers. Chairs were offered so the visitors could sit down and talk to their new friends. One ten-year-old boy brought a bouquet of flowers, presenting it with a well-practiced bow.

Casals picked up a nearby microphone. His voice trembling with emotion, he spoke to everyone in the hall. His English was imperfect, his emotion heartfelt.

Ladies and gentlemen, I assist to one of the most moving scenes that one can see. What we are contemplating has much more importance than it seems. I don't think in any country in the world we could feel such spirit of fraternity and cordiality in its utmost. I feel that in every moment that I have had the privilege of living in this country such proof of heart, of desire of a better world. And this is what has impressed me most in this country. The superlative desire of the highest things in life and how wonderful it is to see that the grown-up people think of the smallest like this is to teach them to begin with the noble feelings, the noble deeds. And one of this is music. To train them to music to make them understand that music is not only sound to have dance or to have small pleasure, but such a high thing in life that perhaps it is music that will save the world.

From behind the stage curtains, Suzuki gulped in surprise. Despite all the goodness that music might bring, even he had never considered that it might be "music that will save the world." The words brought tears to his eyes. What a grand man Pablo Casals was, suggesting to the children and everyone else just how important music was!

Casals continued:

Now I not only congratulate you, the teachers, the grown-up people, but I want to say: my whole admiration, my whole respect and my heartiest congratulations. And another thing that I am happy to say at this moment is that Japan is a great people, and Japan is not only great by its deeds in industrial, in science, in art, but Japan is, I would say the heart of the heart, and this is what humanity needs first, first, first.

As Casals bowed from the stage, his audience rose in

deafening applause. The young musicians on the stage broke into wide smiles, while Shinichi Suzuki moved forward to hug his distinguished guest.

"Thank you, Maestro Casals, your words mean so much to all of us," Shinichi said.

Pablo Casals patted his host's shoulder. "Not as much as the music of these boys and girls meant to me," he whispered.

Chapter Nine

Final Notes

Pablo Casals' praise gave Suzuki new energy and enthusiasm. It also helped to spread word of the music teacher's method to other parts of the world. Many Americans, especially those within the musical community, already knew of the work done by the gentleman from Japan. Japanese Consulate General Mochizuki was among Suzuki's biggest promoters, eagerly sharing the Talent Education Method to anyone who would listen. Some viewed a seven minute film taken at the children's concert in Tokyo, an event that brought together thousands of youngsters from across the country every year to perform. Watching tiny boys and girls play Bach's *Double Violin Concerto* left viewers flabbergasted.

But there were still many skeptics. People still shook their heads at the idea of three and four year olds playing an instrument.

"Children that age should be playing with dolls not

violins," some people declared. "Let the child begin playing an instrument when he is eight or ten, at least."

Other critics blasted the memorization approach that Suzuki used with his very young students. They wondered how students profitted from playing selections without knowing how to read notes.

"We can teach a child to recite the Pledge of Allegiance," observed one music instructor. "But if the child does not know what it means, what good is it?"

The criticisms stung Suzuki. Yet he stood firm in his beliefs, explaining that his students learned to read music as older children. "We know that children in their earliest years learn more than in the rest of their lives," Suzuki declared. "With the right support and encouragement, any young child can find joy and success in learning."

In Japan, his Talent Education institutes dotted the country with classes offered in every sizable city. Over 100 teachers taught his method to thousands of students.

In 1964, Shinichi Suzuki embarked on an important mission. Word of Talent Education had spread to America. There had been talk for years of him bringing a group of students to the United States. Shinichi knew that if his ideas were to gain international acceptance he would have to gain a foothold among American educators. As the leading nation, America's influence could rapidly spread the message throughout the world.

Dr. Robert Klotman was the president of the American String Teachers Association. He and a group of other prominent music teachers invited Shinichi to bring a group of students.

But there was one problem. It would be very expensive to finance a tour of several students. There would be transportation costs, lodging, food, and dozens of other expenses. Shinichi simply did not have enough money. He contacted the American hosts and reminded them that it was Japanese custom for the one who made the invitation to pay for it. So, if the American String Teachers wanted the Japanese children to come visit, they would have to pay.

But the Americans did not have the necessary funds, either. Shinichi decided that he and his students would have a series of fundraising concerts in Japan. They would also raise money at the concerts they gave in America to fund the trip.

Ten students accompanied Shinichi to America. Their ages ranged from five to thirteen. Nine adults, including Shinichi and his wife, traveled with the youngsters. The group planned to rehearse on the trip over, but due to several last minute complications, the young musicians had no practice time before they began their performances.

Their first performance was at the University of Washington in Seattle. They had no time to rest—they were whisked directly from the airport to the concert. Most observers were also unaware that the students came from all over Japan. Some of the students had never even met each other before. Now they were going to play as a unit in concert before their first American audience.

There was no time to worry, however. Pushed in front of the audience, the children played many pieces that had come to be part of the Suzuki repertoire. When the concern ended, the audience, many with tears of sheer joy in their eyes, rose to their feet and gave the shy children a standing ovation. After the concert, Shinichi spoke informally to the excited crowd and answered their questions.

The rest of the tour took the group to many of the most prestigious music schools in America. They visited the Univeristy of Southern Illinois, the New England Conservatory of Music, and the Julliard School of Music. They also presented a concert at the Dag Hammerskjold Auditorium at the United Nations in New York City.

The ultimate goal of the tour was for the students to perform at the Music Educators National Conference in Philadelphia. The ballroom at the Sheraton Hotel was packed with 5,000 curious music teachers. They had heard so much about the revolutionary method developed by Dr. Shinichi Suzuki. Now was their chance to see. Many of the teachers were skeptical. They were prepared to find every slip-up and mistake made by the students.

The first small child was barely visible from the audience. A riser had to be brought out on the stage so she could stand in the audience's view. Shinichi had to lift her onto the riser. She raised her tiny violin and played perfect notes that filled the hall with beautiful music. She was followed by each of the other students. Each played with near perfect tone and deep sensitivity. When the last student finished the difficult *Poeme* by Chauson to close the concert, the audience gave them a standing ovation.

The American reviewers who attended the musical presentations praised the quality of each performance. The evaluators were equally impressed with the behavior of the ten visitors. The young people were energetic and enthusiastic about their music. They also always displayed good manners and respect toward others in the interviews that followed the concerts.

Shinichi spoke at each performance. He also visited unversities and conservatories and talked about his method. His goal was always the same. He wanted to illustrate that children were prized and gifted human beings who needed only to be taught how to become creative and compassionate. "My goal is not to create great muscians," he said over and over, "but to create great people." Professors and pyschologists sought him out for private conferences. Most came away with fresh opinions about the visitor from Japan.

At one post-concert session, Suzuki and a few of his young performers were questioned by American reporters. Again, the issue was raised about "pushing" children into unwanted activities.

"Sounds like Japan must have a lot of stage mommies," one newspaperman quipped.

Before Sukuzi could answer, one of his five-year-old companions stepped forward. "I wanted to play the violin," the youngster declared. "No one pushed a violin at me and ordered me to play. I wanted to."

"This is amazing," declared Julliard School of Music violin instructor Ivan Galamania after hearing the young musicians perform. "They show remarkable training, a wonderful feeling for the rhythm and flow of music."

Dr. Harold Johnson, a music educator from Pennsylvania was also captivated by the performers. "Americans often get the impression that Japanese children are under tremendous pressure to achieve in school," he observed. "But Mr. Suzuki's plan for talent education largely stems from the child's interest in learning, coupled with the active encouragement of parents. Based on the follow-up studies of his former students, they seem to achieve well academically and enjoy the process. We might do well to investigate closely his method for learning and building better character through music."

Music educator Clifford Cook of the Oberlin College Conservatory did exactly that. Once he had researched the program, Cook instituted it at the famous school.

Many other Americans shared Cook's enthuasiam and followed his lead. In fact, Suzuki discovered people who immediately wanted to become teachers using his approach. He shared all he could, promising to send more materials when he returned to Japan. "Please come and visit us," he told people wherever he went. "We welcome visitors to Japan, especially our youngest people. They will play for you with smiles."

More countries invited Suzuki to visit their universities, colleges, and cultural centers. Each time he traveled, he planted seeds of the Talent Education Method. Whether it was England or Switzerland or some little country he had never heard of before, the Japanese music master was happy to carry his message.

Shinichi and his students made another tour of the United States in 1966. This trip was even more successful than the first. They had a full month's schedule of concerts all over the country. This trip so impressed the American string teachers that they began raising money for a group of them to visit Japan to study the Talent Education Method more in-depth.

While Shinichi was excited about the growing popularity of his philosophy there was one problem. There was not a proper place for the teachers visiting Japan to visit. He wanted a building that could house the classrooms and have a hall for performances.

In 1967, the city of Matsumoto decided to help him make this dream come true. Suzuki made money from the tour and used the money to begin work on a building in the city. The city provided him with a large lot directly in front of the city auditorium.

Shinichi made another trip to the United States in the summer of 1967. When he returned, a group of American music teachers accompanied him. The group had returned to attend workshops and to be present at the dedication of the new Talent Education Institute. The teachers and Japanese students played a concert to celebrate the opening of the institute. The new building provided a central location for Shinichi to teach students and to organize the rapidly growing popularity of his philosophy.

Many of the Americans present at the dedication noticed that Suzuki looked tired and fragile. The last few years had been exciting and tiring. They left Japan hoping that he would slow down his pace and find time to rest.

It was not easy for him to slow down, however. By the 1970s, Suzuki was making regular visits to foreign countries. He had found that by taking nine or ten of his students on each trip, he could better demonstrate exactly what he was trying to do. Americans delighted at the junior recitals, programs always beginning with "Twinkle, Twinkle, Little Star" and moving quickly into more difficult selections. The children basked in the attention, enjoying every moment.

As the popularity of his method grew, so did the possibilty that it could be misunderstood. Word spread to Japan that some teachers did not properly understand Talent Education, but were nevertheless claiming to use it in their instruction. They did not stress the importance of tonalization or of proper posture when they taught. These poorly trained teachers were hurting Talent Education's reputation.

Shinichi needed a way to instruct teachers in his method. His supporters in America also saw the need and began looking for a way to help. They convinced the New York State Council of Arts to give the famous Eastman School of Music in Rochester, New York, a grant to train teachers. Soon music educators from all over the country were coming to Eastman to learn the ways of Talent Education.

It was also important to develop a repertoire of songs for the Suzuki method curriculum. It took many years to organize the ten books of music that would comprise the violin course. First the music had to be written or selected, and then it was organized in the correct order. Each piece had to develop skills that were learned in previous songs, while introducing the student to a new technique on the violin. The goal was to create a set of songs that gradually developed the talents of the students.

The Talent Education model was not used only with the violin, of course. It could be applied to all instruments. Soon there was a Suzuki repertoire for piano, viola, cello, guitar, and flute. But most importantly, Shinichi insisted that his way of education could be used throughout a child's education.

As the number of well-trained Talent Education teachers increased, the number of students increased, too. In the summer of 1971, the University of Wisconsin held the first Suzuki Institute. Students from all over the country traveled to the campus to attend a week of classes.

By 1976 there were nearly twenty Suzuki Institutes located all over the country. In 1972 the Suzuki Association of the Americas was formed to oversee the development of teachers and institutes.

Despite the growth of Talent Education in America, no recital was more highly anticipated than the annual gathering in Tokyo. The sight and sound of 3,000 young people sliding their bows across violin strings left those in the audience in awe. The program featured soloists, small groups, and the entire ensemble. By the end of the presentation, those attending were on their feet, applauding and cheering.

In 1970, the Japanese children took another trip. This time they visited the great capitals of Europe. They returned to the place where the beautiful music they played had originated. Shinichi could not accompany the children on this trip. His wife, Waltraud, who also acted as an interpreter, replaced him. The first stop on the trip was Berlin, Waltraud's home town. How many years it had been since she had first sung for the young Japanese music student! So much had happened in the intervening years. The war, the suffering, and now this message of Talent Education that her husband had brought to the world.

The European tour was very successful. The students traveled from Berlin to London, then to Paris, and onto Lisbon. They were greeted by standing ovations and enthusiastic reviews in every city.

As one decade slipped into another, Shinichi Suzuki expanded his mission to help children. Convinced that Talent Education could reach into other areas of life, he made special efforts to reach primary school principals. He did not want one single student to fail in school. He also emphasized the need for mentally retarded children to be reached. Although he still held the parents as the most important factor in fostering talent among young people, he challenged politicians and government leaders to do their part.

In his eighties, Suzuki decided to put his ideas about fostering creativity in the young into a book called *Nurtured by Love*. His wife, Waltraud, translated the manuscript into English. "She always understood the language better than I did," the music master said, smiling.

Then it was off to another concert, another tour. Invitations arrived daily along with fan letters from all over the world, written with dedication and care by young violin students and appreciators of Suzuki's efforts.

"The future of the world belongs to the young," Suzuki told one audience of educators in 1989. "Because they do not have the voice to speak for themselves, we must recognize their needs. The world will be more peaceful and happy if we do."

Suzuki found a personal kind of peace and happiness in painting. He spent hours at a time using a brush to deftly create a picture. "We should have an exhibit of your work," one friend suggested.

Flattered, Suzuki shook his head. Painting was a private activity in which he could retreat with his own thoughts and create in solitude. "I am afraid there would be many people who would say I should have stayed with music," he joked. "Very likely, I would be first among those people."

If his painting impressed some of his friends and associates, his listening skills amazed them even more. He could listen to a tape of a young person playing the violin and then describe every movement of the performer, good and bad. Each observation was based solely on listening to a tape. He could even discuss the performer's character traits, along with their strengths and weaknesses of behavior.

"It is uncanny," observed one of Suzuki's associates. "After the tape has been returned, we would hear that Master Suzuki was right about everything."

The ever modest music teacher simply shook his head at such compliments. "I have been doing this for a long time," he explained. He also gave much credit to *kan,* "intuition" or a sixth sense. "Just as one tunes an instrument for good sound, one tunes the ear. Let us say my hearing is my strongest sense. By now, it probably should be."

As the years passed and the number of young people learning music through the Suzuki Method grew even larger, the music teacher slowed down. He no longer had the strength to visit the classroom and teach. Now his movements were feeble and calculated. For as long as he could, Suzuki traveled, always willing to share his knowledge.

Yet the trips took their toll. Gradually, Waltraud stepped in to take her husband's place, although she knew no one could truly do that. Only Shinichi Suzuki could lift minds and spirits to his method. But his wife carried his good wishes to all she met.

Then, as he slipped into his nineties, Suzuki spent more and more time within the boundaries of his home in Matsumoto. Teachers and friends stopped by to visit him. Some days he was strong enough to receive them. Other times, his wife kindly gave his apologies. No one complained. The man who had given so much to so many was simply tiring out.

Despite the infirmities of old age, Suzuki maintained a positive attitude that he shared with others. He knew there were many people who knew the end of life was within sight and felt they had accomplished little in the years they had lived. He drew advice from his longtime mentor in music, Mozart. "I live in the love of everyone. Only this life is worth living."

On Monday, January 26, 1998, that life so worth living ended. Shinichi Suzuki died at the age of ninety-nine. Around the world, people mourned the death of the beloved music teacher.

"Shinichi Suzuki was a unique individual," wrote one American newspaper editor. "He was driven by a passion to bring a special joy to boys and girls, and to make them better people. Convinced that talent could be fostered within any child, he dedicated his life to promoting that cause. Biologically, he had no children of his own. In every other sense, he had thousands."

At the time of his death, there were over 400,000 young children studying the violin, cello, piano and flute, and utilizing the Suzuki Method. Those students lived in over forty different countries scattered around the world. Some 25,000 boys and girls were studying music by the Suzuki Method in Japan alone.

In October of 1998, during what would have been the 100th birthday anniversary of the music teacher from Japan, countries around the world honored Suzuki with special concerts. In England, Argentina, Brazil, Germany and, of course, Japan—junior Suzuki musicians took to the stage to play. One hundred twenty-five cities in the United States held performances in his honor. Small hands gripped bows that slipped and slid along miniature instruments. Music filled the air, offering a loving legacy to a gentle man from Japan.

Timeline

1888—Masakichi Suzuki, Shinichi's father, begins to make violins.

1898—Shinichi Suzuki born in Nagoya, Japan, in October.

1913—Enters Nagoya Community School.

1916—Graduates and begins to work in Suzuki Violin factory.

1920—Goes to Europe with the Marquis Tokugawa in October.

1928—Marries Waltraud Prange on February 8. Returns to Japan four months later. Mother dies.

1929—Forms Suzuki String Quartet with brothers.

1930—Moves to Tokyo, Japan.

1937—Appointed to teach at the Imperial Music School in Tokyo.

1943—Waltraud moves to Hakone. Shinichi produces lumber in Kiso-Fukushima.

1944—Father dies January 31. Koji Toyoda comes to live.

1945—Begins Talent Education Program at Matsumoto Music School.

1952—Koji leaves for Paris.

1955—First Annual Talent Education Concert held in Tokyo on March 30.

1961—Pablo Casals attends Talent Education Concert in Tokyo on April 16.

1964—First American tour of Suzuki's students.

1969—*Nurtured by Love*, translated by Waltraud Suzuki, becomes available to English readers.

1970—First group of American Suzuki Method students tour Japan.

1978—Celebrates fiftieth wedding anniversary on February 18.

1998—Dies on January 26 at ninety-nine years old.

Bibliography

Cook, Clifford A. *A Story of Talent Training from Japan.* Smithtown, NY: Exposition Press, 1980.

Fox, Susannah. "Fine music, a beautiful art" *U.S. News & World Report*, February 9, 1998, p. 12.

Johnson, Robert Leland. *Super Babies: A Handbook of Enriched and Accelerated Childhood Development.* Smithtown, NY: Exposition Press, 1982.

Kendell, John D. *The Suzuki Violin Method in American Music Education.* Washington, D.C.: MENC, 1973.

"Shinich Suzuki." *The New Grove Dictionary of Music and Musicians,* London: MacMillan Publishers Limited, 1980. Volume 18, pp. 386-387.

"Shinichi Suzuki Dies at 99" (obituary) *The New York Times,* January 27, 1998, A17.

"Suzuki method founder; taught kids to play violin" (obituary) *Chicago Tribune*, January 27, 1998, Section 2, p. 8.

Suzuki, Shinichi. (translated by Waltraud Suzuki). *Nurtured by Love: A New Approach to Education.* Smithtown, NY: Exposition Press, 1969.

Websites

A Memorial: Dr. Shinichi Suzuki: 1898-1998
mr.data.com/fandrich/eric/suzuki/front.htm

Suzuki Association of the Americas
www.suzukiassociation.org

Index